French - Slovak

LEARNING FLASHCARDS

FOR BABIES TODDLERS

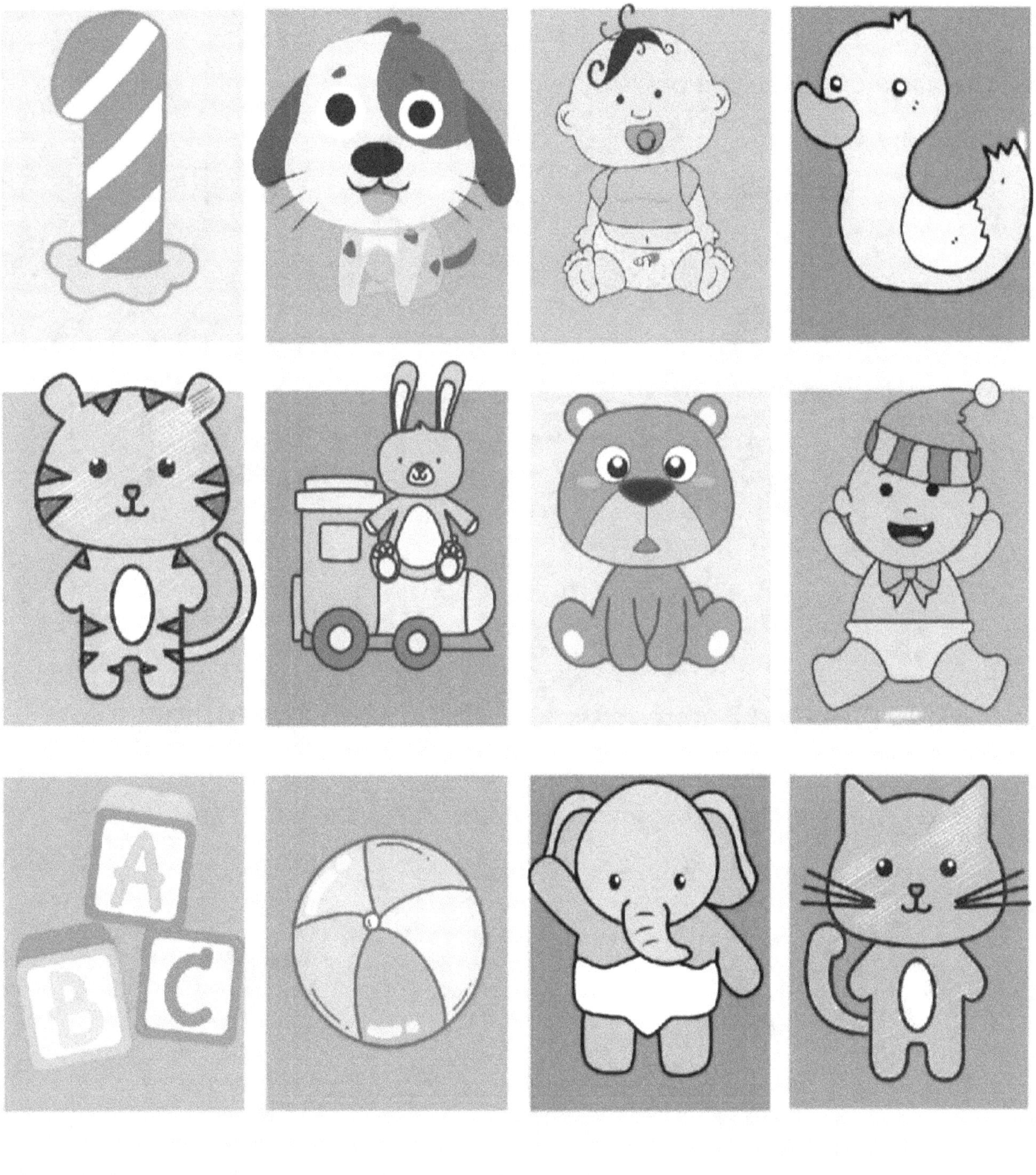

alligator

aligátor

The alligator is having a party.

fourmi

mravec

The ant is red.

ours

medveď

The bear loves you.

abeille

včela

The bee is saying hello.

oiseau

vták

The bird is flying.

papillon

motýľ

The butterfly is pretty.

chameau

ťava

The camel has a hump.

chat

mačka

The cat is happy.

dinosaure

dinosaurus

The dinosaur is laying eggs.

poulet

kura

The chicken is dancing.

vache

krava

The cow has a bell.

cerf

jeleň

The reindeer has a toy.

chien

pes

The dog has two floppy ears.

dauphin

delfín

The dolphin is swimming.

canard

kačica

The duck has a bow.

aigle

orol

The eagle is looking for food.

l'éléphant

slon

The elephant is sitting.

poisson

ryby

The fish is a clownfish.

libellule

vážka

The dragonfly is blue.

renard

líška

The fox has a red nose.

grenouille

žaba

The frog is smiling.

girafe

žirafa

The giraffe has a long neck.

chèvre

koza

The goat has a beard

ver de terre

červ

The worm is in the apple

poule

sliepky

The hen has chicks.

hippopotame

hroch

The hippo is big.

cheval

kôň

The horse is fast.

kangourou

klokan

The kangaroo has a baby.

chaton

mačiatko

The kitten is playing.

lion

lev

The lion has a mane.

homard

homár

The lobster is red.

singe

opice

The monkey has a tail.

poulpe

chobotnica

The octopus has food.

hibou

sova

The owls have big eyes.

panda

panda

The panda wears a diaper.

porc

prasa

The pig is fat and pink.

chiot

šteňa

The dog is brown.

lapin

králik

The rabbit has a carrot.

rat

potkan

The mouse is writing something.

crabe

krab

The crab has two pinchers.

requin

žralok

The shark is scary.

mouton

ovce

The sheep are very fluffy.

escargot

slimák

The snail is slow.

serpent

had

The snake has poison.

araignée

pavúk

The spider is purple.

écureuil

veverička

The squirrel has a nut.

tigre

tiger

The tiger has a red bow.

tortue

korytnačka

The turtle has a shell.

loup

vlk

The wolf is smiling.

zèbre

zebra

The zebra is black and white.

dinde

moriak

The turkey has two legs.

coq

kohút

The rooster will crow.

perroquet

papagáj

The parrot is colorful.

hérisson

ježko

The hedgehog has apples.

pomme

jablko

The apple has a leaf.

abricot

marhuľa

The apricot is yellow.

avocat

avokádo

The avocado has a nut.

banane

banán

The banana is yellow.

la mûre

ostružina

There are a lot of blackberries.

cassis

čierna ríbezľa

The blackcurrants are yummy.

myrtille

čučoriedka

The blueberries are sweet.

cerise

čerešňa

The cherries have a stem.

noix de coco

kokosový orech

The coconuts have juice.

figues

figy

The fig has seeds.

grain de raisin

zrnko vína

The grapes are purple.

pamplemousse

grapefruit

The grapefruits are sour.

kiwi

kiwi

The kiwi is fresh.

citron

citrón

The lemons are yellow.

citron vert

vápno

We have lots of lime.

litchi

liči

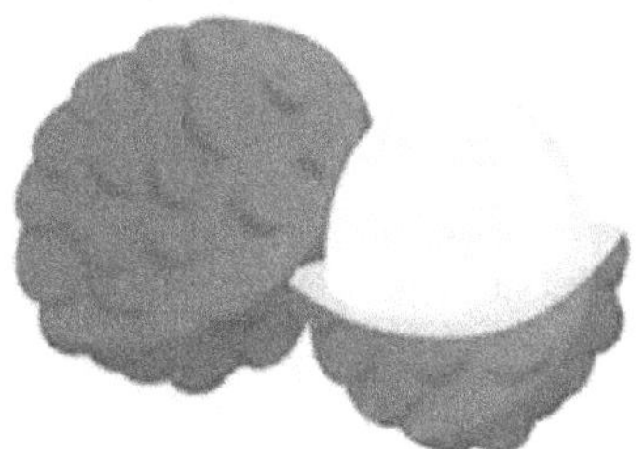

I like to eat lychee.

mandarine

mandarínková oranžová

Oranges are refreshing.

mangue

mango

Mango is my favorite fruit.

orange

oranžový

Mandarins are like oranges.

papaye

papája

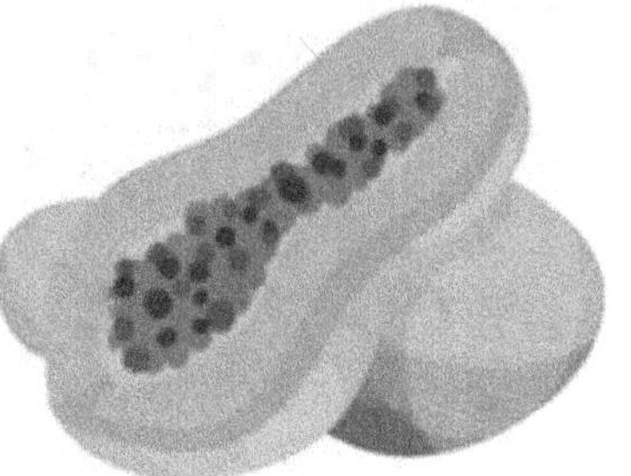

Papayas have lots of seeds.

pêche

broskyňa

Peaches are juicy.

poire

hruška

Pears have a strange figure.

ananas

ananás

The pineapple has a thumbs up.

prune

slivka

Plums are healthy for you.

Pomegranates are all red.

The raspberry is shiny.

The strawberry has leaves on top.

The watermelon is big.

The tangerine looks like an orange.

I like to eat apple pie.

gâteau

torta

That cake is huge.

bonbons

cukrík

Candy is not good for your teeth.

biscuit

sušienka

Cookies are easy to make.

donut

šiška

I like strawberry donuts.

crème glacée

zmrzlina

The ice cream is melting.

muffin

muffin

The muffin has a cute wrapper.

pudding

puding

We eat pudding on Christmas.

classeur

zakladač

I keep pictures in my binder.

livre

kniha

I like to eat books.

sac à dos

batoh

The backpack has lots of stuff.

les ciseaux

nožnice

I have scissors in my bag.

épingles

pins

Pins can hold stuff up.

agrafe

klip

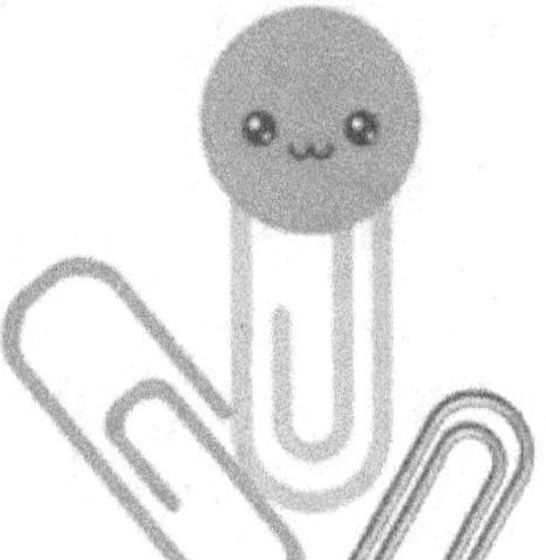

Clips can hold up paper.

papier

papier

I have lots of paper.

agrafeuse

zošívačka

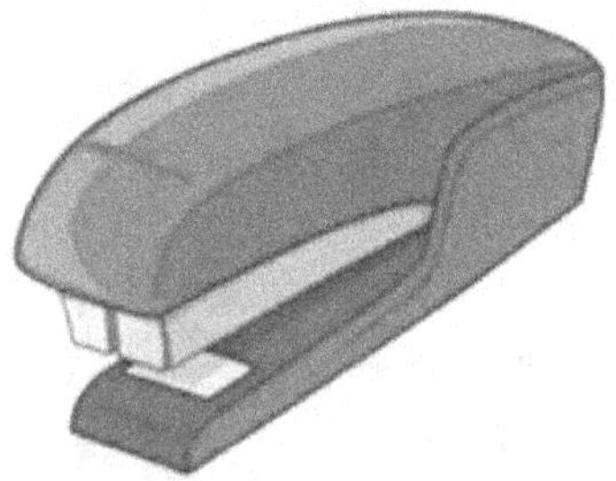

My stapler is shiny and red.

calculatrice

kalkulačka

My calculator has buttons.

règle

pravítko

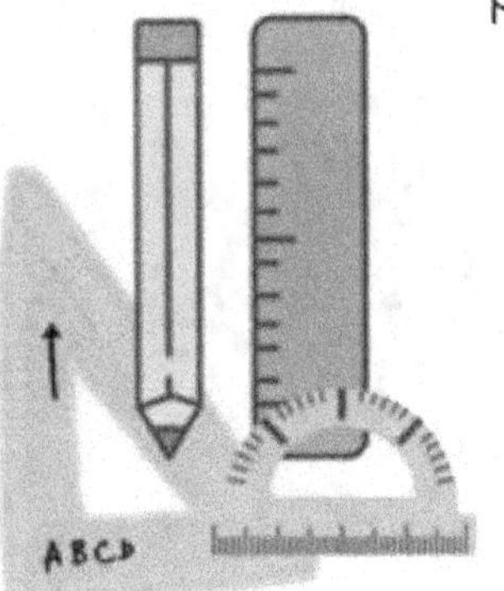

I have lots of rulers.

la colle

lepidlo

The glue is sticky.

bibliothèque

knižnica

My bookcase has lots of things.

calendrier

kalendár

I have a calendar on my table.

chaise

stoličky

My chair is fancy.

l'horloge

hodiny

The clock says that it's 3 o'clock.

ordinateur

počítačový

I do things on my computer.

bureaux

stoly

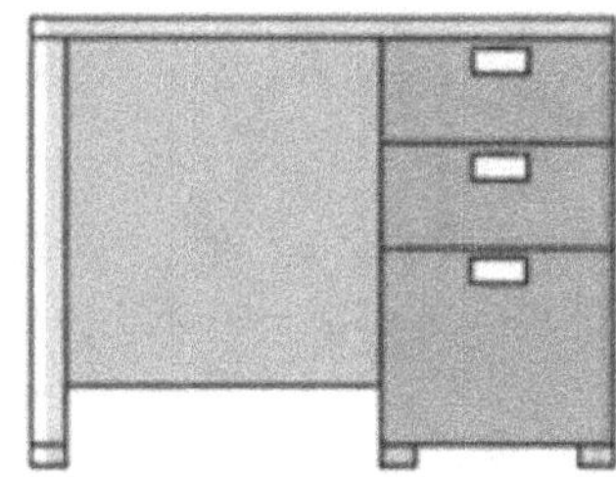

I put lots of things on my desk.

dictionnaire

slovník

The dictionary has lots of words.

la gomme

guma

Erasers are used with pencils.

carte

pre

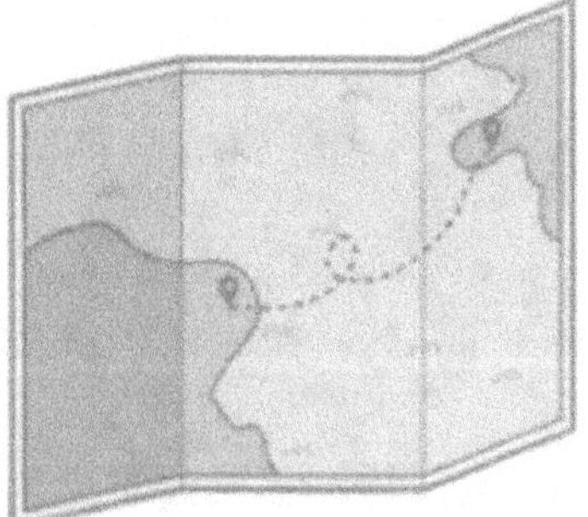

The map shows you different places.

carnet

zápisník

I use notebooks at school.

stylo

pero

My pen is very pretty.

crayon

ceruzka

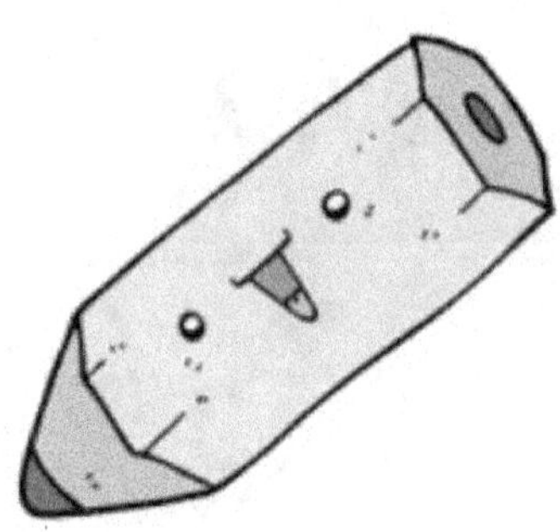

My friend gave me a pencil.

ceinture

remeň

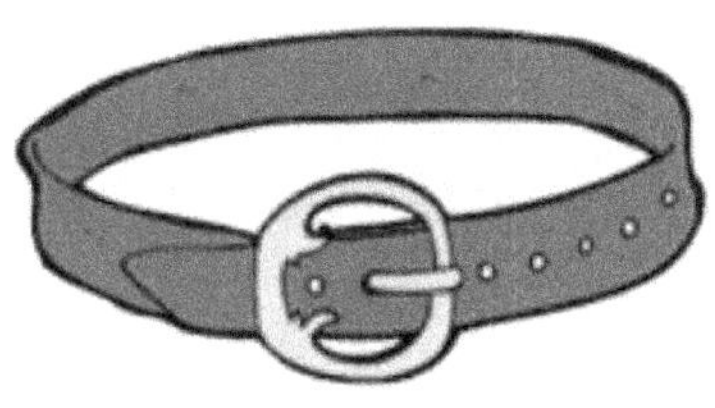

I have a belt on my pants.

bottes

topánky

I have big brown boots.

chapeau

klobúk

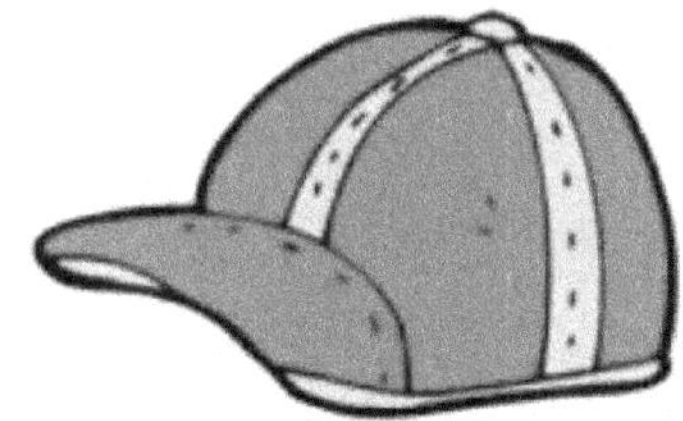

My mom bought me a new cap.

manteau

kabát

She has a long yellow coat.

robes

šaty

My dress has a bow.

gants

rukavice

I got new gloves.

chapeau

klobúk

That hat is for a wicked witch.

veste

bunda

The jacket is cozy.

jeans

džínsy

My jeans are long.

pyjamas

pyžamá

I sleep in my pajamas.

un pantalon

nohavice

The bear is wearing pants.

imperméable

pláštenka

We wear our raincoats when it is raining.

écharpe

šál

The baby has a scarf around his neck.

chemise

košele

I like this shirt the best.

des chaussures

topánky

I have red and blue shoes.

jupe

sukne

My skirt has lots of buttons.

pantalon

dlhé nohavice

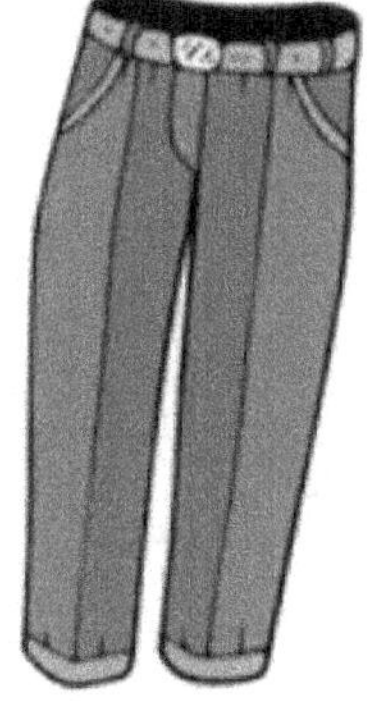

My dad wears slacks.

chaussons

papuče

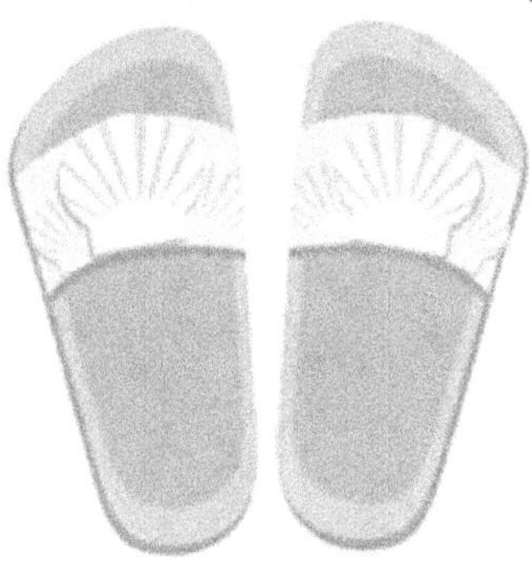

I have seashells on my sandals.

chaussettes

ponožky

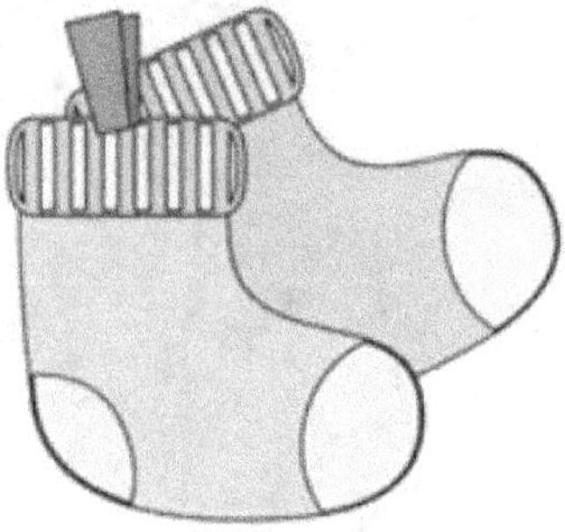

My baby sister wears socks.

costume

oblek

My brother is wearing a suit.

chandail

sveter

I am wearing a sweater for winter.

cravate

viazanka

My dad wears a tie to meetings.

pantalon

nohavice

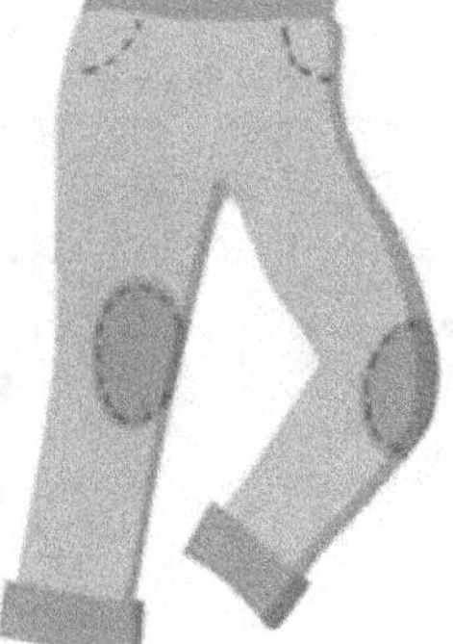

The trousers look like jeans.

slip

spodky

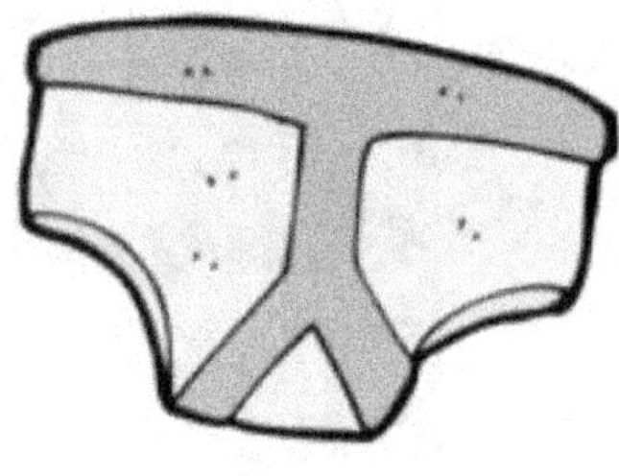

I always wear my underwear.

maillot de corps

nátelník

My undershirt has a star.

une

jeden

Number one and the bee are friends.

deux

dva

The cat and the mouse both love two.

trois

tri

The bear gives number three a present.

quatre

štyri

Number four is a home for the cat.

cinq

päť

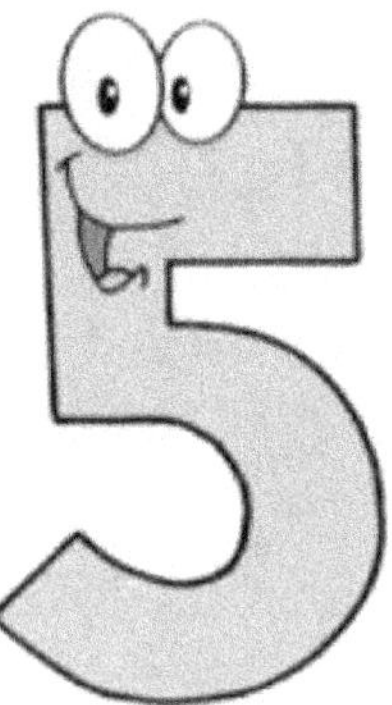

Number five hatches an egg.

six

šesť

Number six is going to eat a carrot.

sept

sedem

Number seven is playing with the tiger.

huit

osem

Number eight is funny.

neuf

deväť

Number nine meets the parrot.

dix

desať

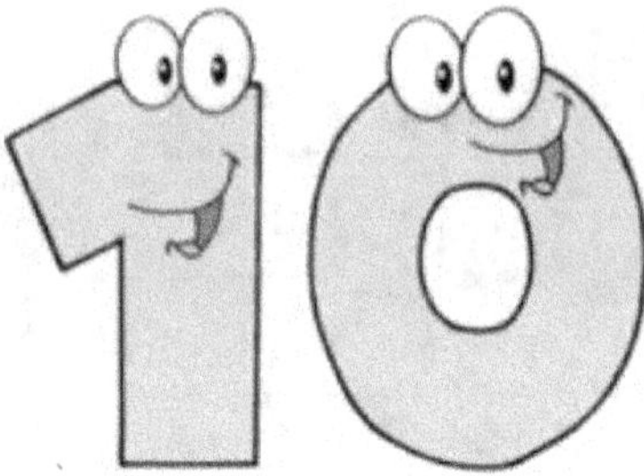

Number ten is smiling.

onze

jedenásť

Number eleven has big eyes.

douze

dvanásť

Number twelve is number one and two.

treize

trinásť

Number thirteen is excited.

quatorze

štrnásť

The number fourteen is vast.

quinze

pätnásť

The number fifteen is green.

seize

šestnásť

Sixteen is my lucky number.

dix-sept

sedemnásť

Number seventeen look alike.

dix-huit

osemnásť

Number eighteen will go to the circus.

dix-neuf

devätnásť

I am nineteen now!

vingt

dvadsať

Number twenty has a zero.

fourmi

mravec

The ant has lots of legs.

cloche

zvon

The bell will ring.

vache

krava

The cow has a bow.

poupée

bábika

She has a cute bear doll.

oeuf

vajíčko

The chick has hatched out of the egg.

poisson

ryby

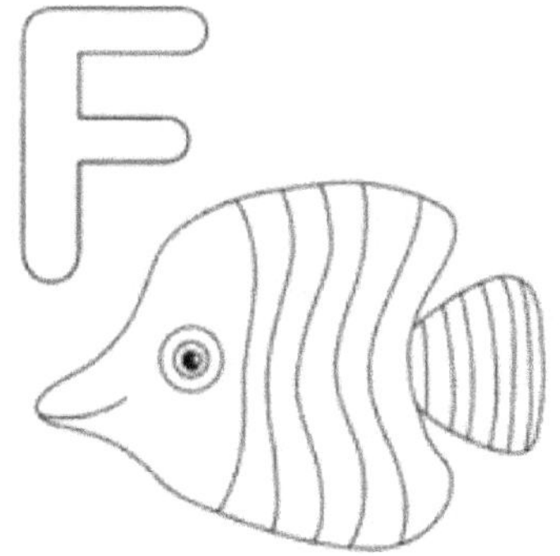

The fish is swimming in the water.

chèvre

koza

The goat is sitting on the grass.

chapeau

klobúk

He is wearing a hat.

crème glacée

zmrzlina

I like to eat ice cream.

confiture

džem

The kitten is sitting on the jam jar.

chaton

mačiatko

The cat is sleeping on the floor.

lion

lev

The lion is waiting for the tiger.

rat

potkan

The mouse has lots of presents.

nez

nos

The reindeer has a red nose.

hibou

sova

The owl is sleeping.

porc

prasa

The pig will eat cupcakes.

reine

kráľovná

The queen has a big crown.

lapin

králik

The rabbit is jumping up and down.

mouton

ovce

The sheep have fluffy wool.

tortue

korytnačka

The turtle has a shell.

parapluie

dáždnik

The mouse is holding an umbrella.

van

van

The van is driving along the road.

pastèque

vodný melón

The watermelon has lots of seeds.

xylophone

xylofón

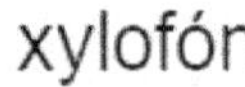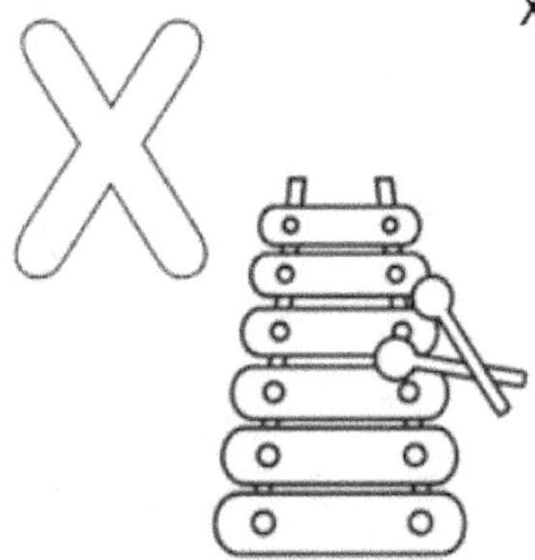

We are going to play the
xylophone.

yaourt

jogurt

We opened the yogurt can.

zèbre

zebra

The zebra is surprised.

rose

ružová

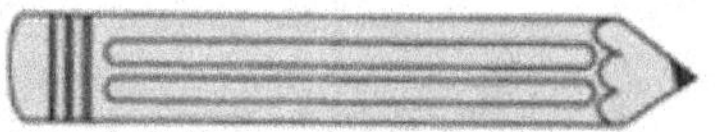

color the word and
the picture in pink

Most of my clothes are pink.

marron

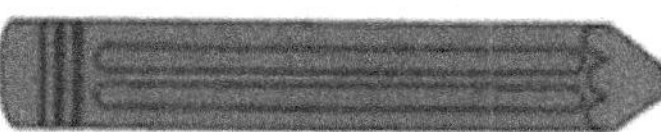

hnedý

color the word and
the picture in pink

My chocolate is brown.

gris

šedá

color the word and
the picture in pink

I don't like the color gray.

vert

zelená

color the word and
the picture in pink

The vegetables are green.

jaune

žltá

color the word and
the picture in pink

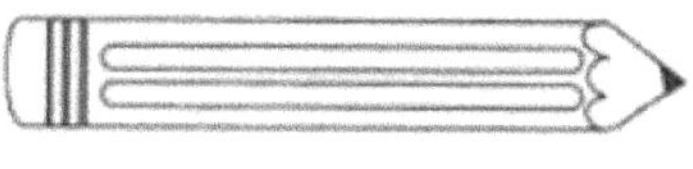

Bananas are yellow.

blanc

biely

color the word and
the picture in pink

The paper that I write on is white.

rouge

červená

color the word and
the picture in pink

Apples are red.

bleu

modrá

color the word and
the picture in pink

The night sky is blue.

percer

vŕtačka

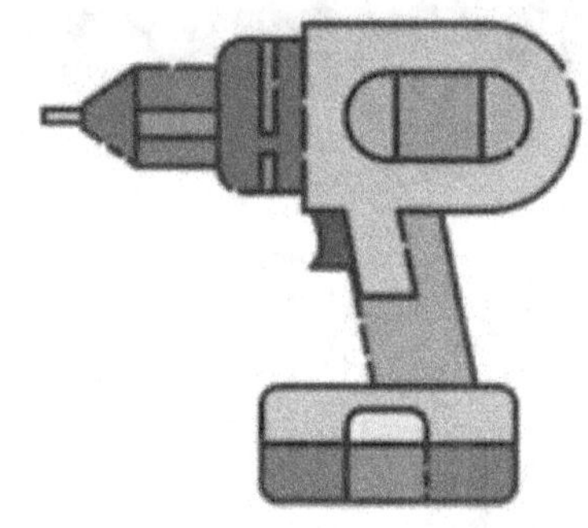

The drill will help us fix this.

marteau

kladivo

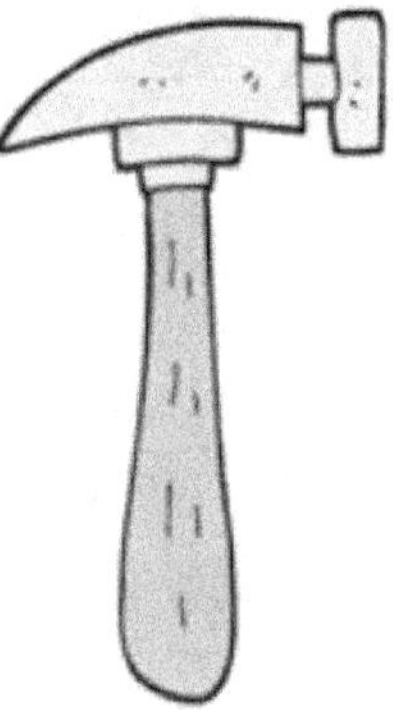

The hammer is going to nail the picture.

couteau

nôž

The knife is sharp.

pinces

kliešte

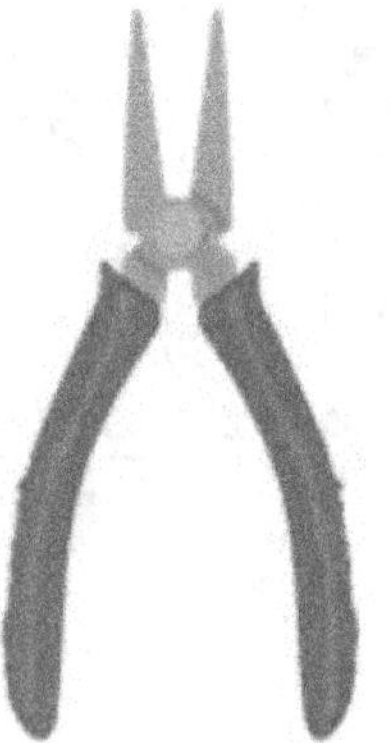

The plier is used for many things.

vu

pílka

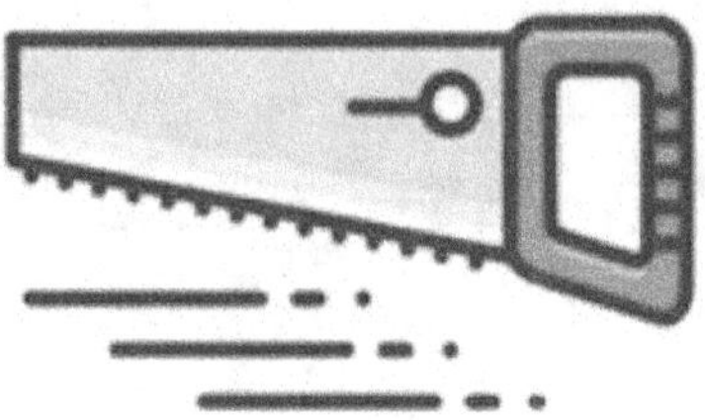

The saw can chop wood.

les ciseaux

nožnice

I use scissors to cut paper.

tournevis

skrutkovač

The screwdriver can screw in the knots.

clé

vyvrtnutie

The wrench can help unscrew the knots.

avion

lietadlo

The airplane is going to leave now.

vélo

bicykel

The bicycle is beautiful.

bateau

čln

The boat is floating on the water.

autobus

autobus

The bus is going to school.

voiture

auto

The car is green.

hélicoptère

vrtuľník

The helicopter is looking for something.

cheval

kôň

You can ride the horse.

jet

tryska

The jet is high-speed.

moto

motocykel

The motorcycle is on the road.

navire

loď

The ship is on the water.

métro

metro

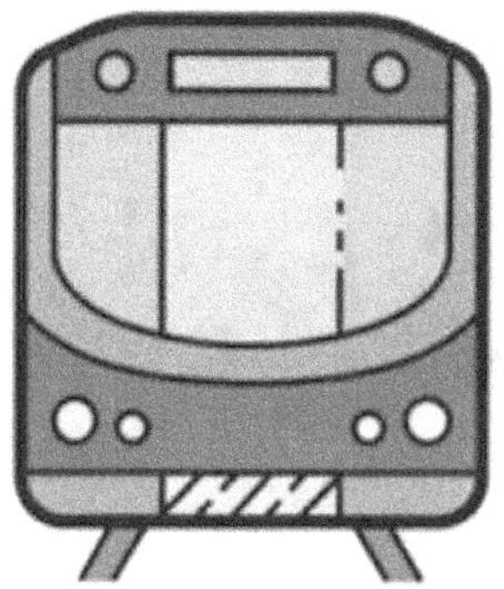

My mom goes on the subway to work.

taxi

taxi

The taxi has someone inside.

train

vlak

The train is going slowly.

un camion

nákladné auto

The truck has stuff in it.

asperges

špargľa

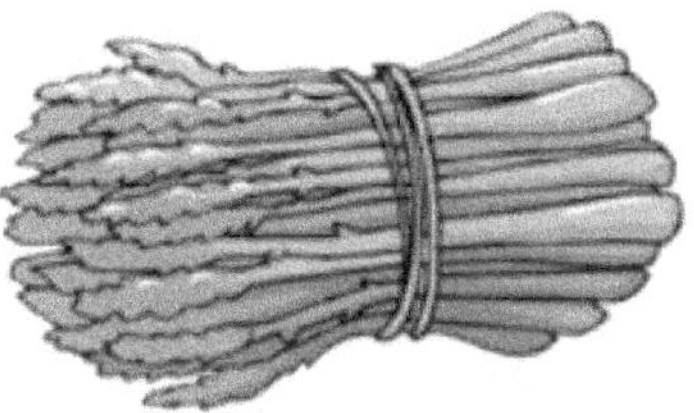

The asparagus is in a bundle.

des haricots

fazuľa

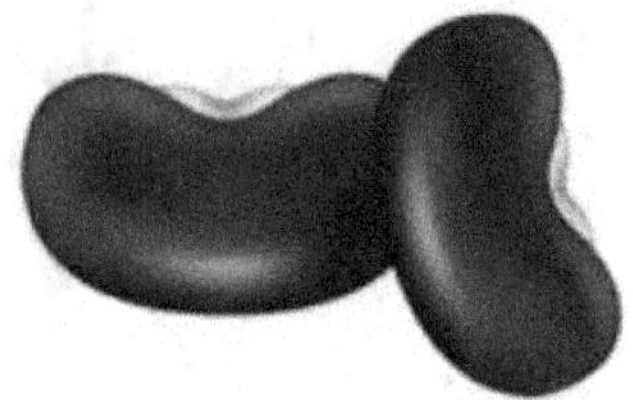

The beans are smooth.

brocoli

brokolica

The broccoli is dancing.

chou

kapusta

Bunnies like to eat cabbage.

carotte

mrkva

The carrots are very long.

céleri

zeler

The celery has lots of leaves.

blé

kukurica

Corn soup is delicious.

concombre

uhorka

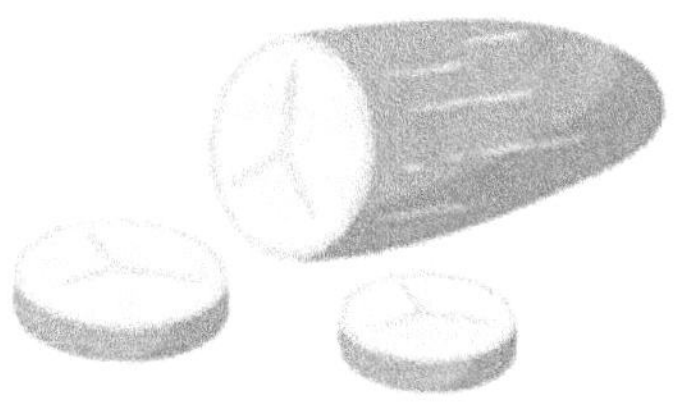

The cucumbers are cut into pieces.

aubergine

baklažán

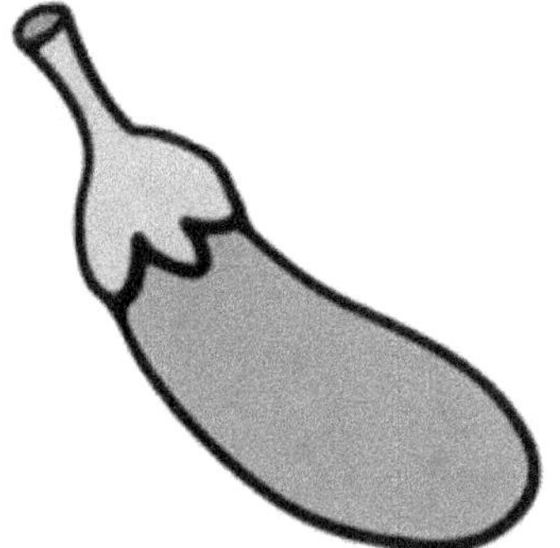

The eggplant is purple.

poivre vert

zelené korenie

The green pepper is juicy.

salade

šalát

The lettuce is all green.

oignon

cibuľa

The onions make my eyes water.

pois

hrach

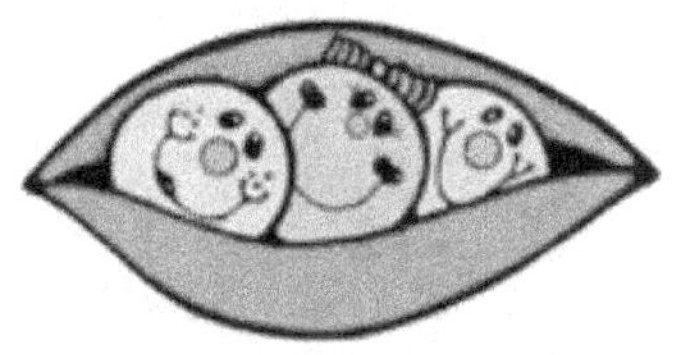

The peas are all in a pod.

patate

zemiak

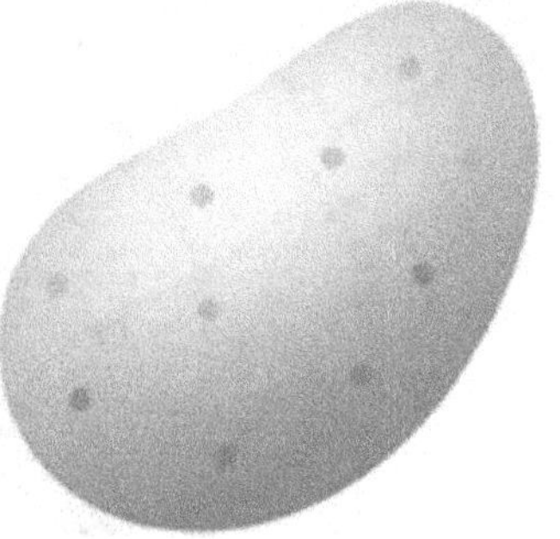

The potato is very shiny.

citrouille

tekvica

The pumpkin is for Halloween.

un radis

reďkev

The radish is a type of vegetable.

épinard

špenát

The spinach is good with cheese.

patate douce

sladký zemiak

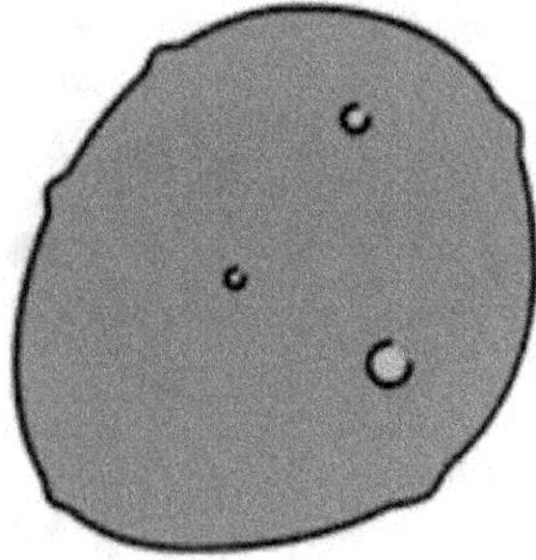

The sweet potato is quite sweet.

tomate

paradajka

I don't like to eat tomatoes.

navet

kvaka

My mom bought some turnips.

nuageux

zakalený

The weather is cloudy today.

du froid

chladný

I like cold weather.

cool

chladný

The temperature is cold today.

brumeux

hmlistý

The fog is so strong I can't see the city.

chaud

horúco

The fire is burning hot.

humide

vlhký

It's so humid and wet today.

pluvieux

daždivý

It's raining very hard.

neigeux

zasnežený

Welcome to snow land!

orageux

búrlivý

I hate the stormy weather.

ensoleillé

slnečno

The sun is shining!

chaud

teplý

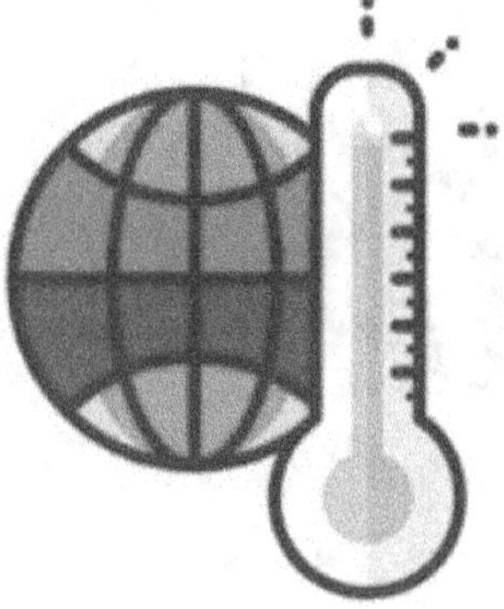

The whole world is warm today!

venteux

veterno

The leaves are blowing away since it's so windy!

tante

teta

My aunt is very nice to me.

frère

brat

My brother is very fun to play with.

cousin

bratranec

I love going to the playground with my cousin.

fille

dcéra

I like to read books with my daughter.

père

otec

My father is playing with me.

petite fille

vnučka

My granddaughter has blond hair.

grand-mère

babička

My grandmother is very old and has glasses.

petit fils

vnuk

My grandson and I are very excited today!

mère

matka

My mother likes to pick me up.

neveu

synovec

My father's nephew is my cousin.

nièce

neter

My niece is very good at playing ball.

sœur

sestra

My sister is so pretty!

fils

syn

My son likes to play with toy cars.

belle fille

nevlastná dcéra

My stepdaughter likes the color orange.

belle-mère

nevlastná matka

My stepmother is pretty.

beau-fils

nevlastný syn

This is my stepson, Greg.

oncle

strýko

My uncle tells lots of funny jokes.

bol

miska

The bowl has nothing inside.

tasse

pohár

My mom drinks her coffee out of a cup.

plat

jedlo

That dish has a bone inside.

fourchette

vidlička

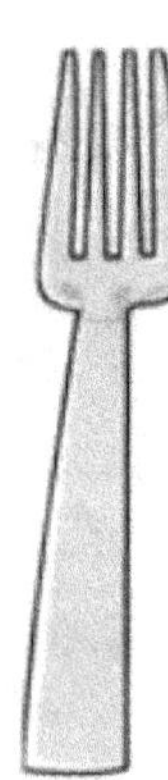

We have more spoons than forks.

verre

sklo

I have a glass of water on my desk.

couteau

nôž

I have a knife in my kitchen.

agresser

džbánik

This mug of coffee is for my dad.

serviette de table

obrúsok

You can use the napkins to clean your hands.

poivre

korenie

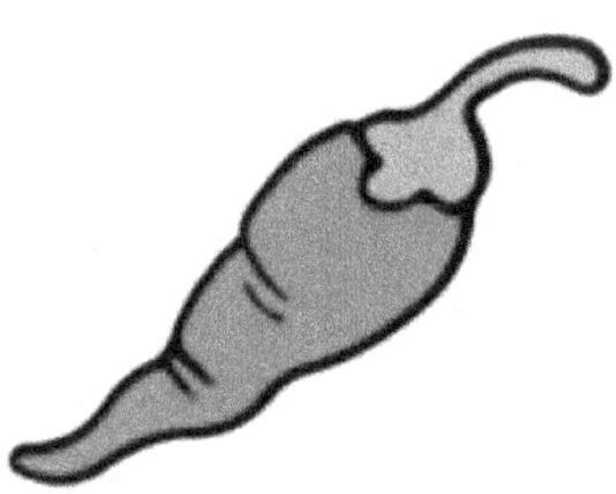

The pepper is very spicy.

lanceur

džbán

Pour yourself some lemonade from the pitcher.

assiette

tanier

Can you help me wash the plates?

salade

šalát

The salad is very healthy for you.

sel

soľ

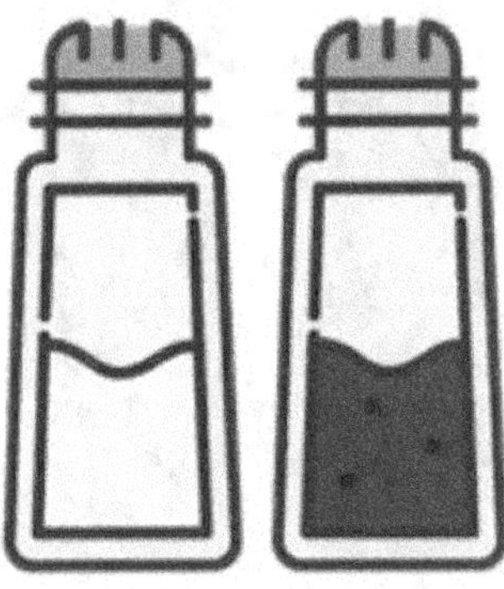

The salt tastes good with a few pinches of pepper.

soucoupe

podšálka

The plate is for my cup.

cuillère

lyžice

I use a spoon to eat my rice.

sucre

cukor

The pack of sugar is very heavy.

dimanche

nedeľa

Sunday

Sunday is the day to go to Church!

lundi

pondelok

Monday

Monday is the day to start school.

mardi

utorok

Tuesday

We will go to the shops on Tuesday.

mercredi

streda

Wednesday

Wednesday is hard to spell!

jeudi

štvrtok

Thursday

Thursday is the fourth day of the week!

vendredi

piatok

Friday

My birthday is on Friday!

samedi

sobota

Saturday

Saturday is the weekend!

cuire

upiecť

The chef will bake a cake.

ébullition

variť

I will boil the eggs.

griller

grilovať

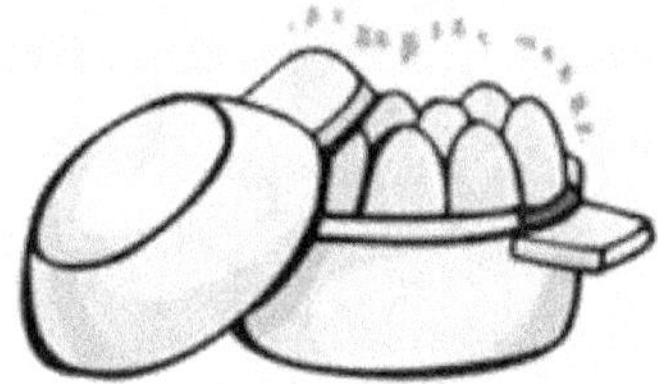

Broil is very yummy.

ouvre-boîte

otvárač na konzervy

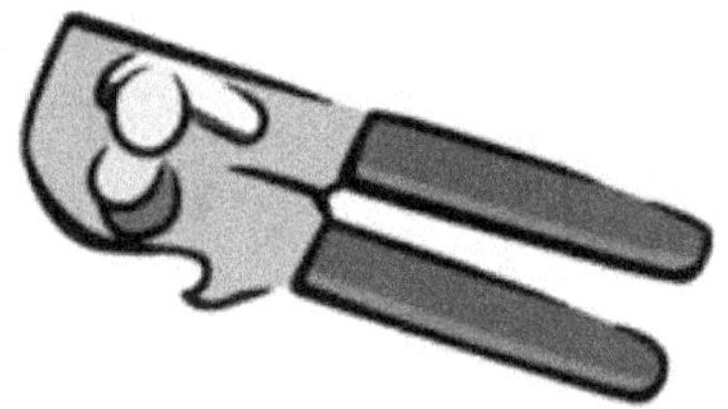

That can opener is used for opening cans.

frire

poter

The pan can fry lots of things.

gril

gril

We have a grill in our backyard.

tasse à mesurer

odmerka

My mom uses the measuring cup for baking.

cuillère à mesurer

odmerná lyžica

I use a measuring spoon to eat my dessert.

four micro onde

mikrovlnná rúra

The microwave is used to heat food.

bol à mélanger

misa na miešanie

She is using the mixing bowl to mix things.

serviettes en papier

papierové uteráky

Dry your hands with paper towels.

poché aux œufs

vaječný kôš

The poach is put on noodles.

porte pot

držiak hrncov

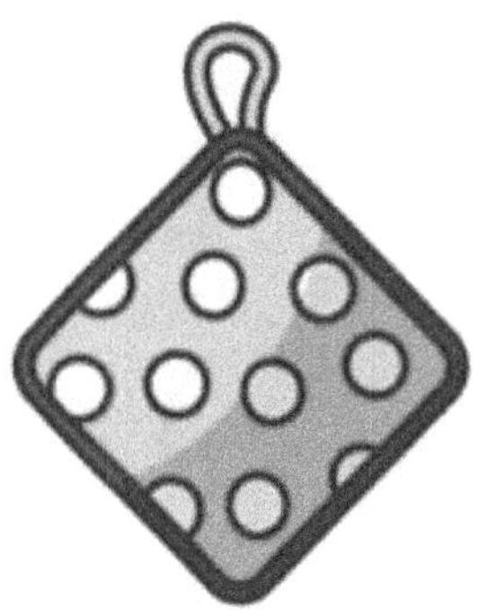

The potholder is soft.

rôti

pečienka

The chef made roast chicken.

rouleau à pâtisserie

valček

He is holding a rolling pin.

brouiller

zhon

My mom is making scrambled eggs for breakfast.

mijoter

vrieť

The simmer is rice today.

couteau

nôž

The knife is sharp.

cuillère

lyžice

I eat my food with a spoon and fork.

spatule

špachtľa

The spatula will help us flip the steak over.

vapeur

parný

The steam is coming from the pot.

passoire

cedidlo

The strainer is used to strain stuff.

minuteur

časomerač

I set my timer for 12:00.

fourchette

vidlička

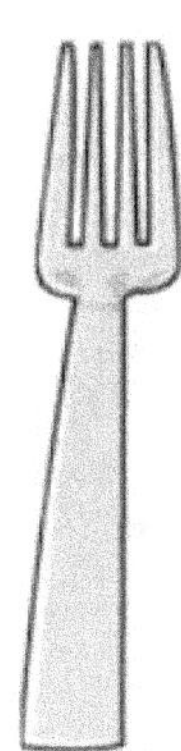

I have lots of metallic forks.

grille-pain

opekač hrianok

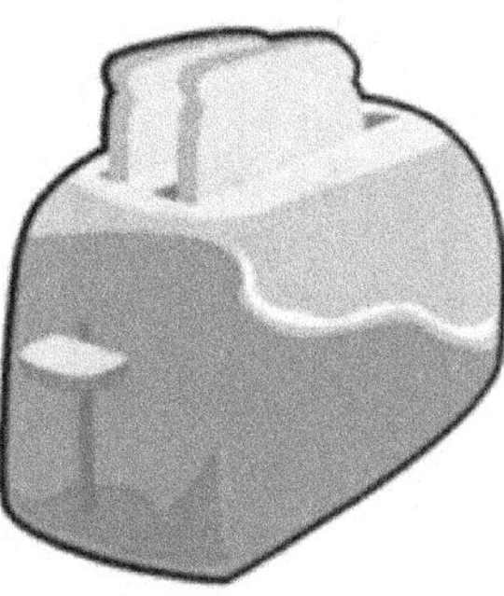

The toaster will toast my bread.

bouilloire

kanvice

The kettle has tea inside.

réfrigérateur

chladnička

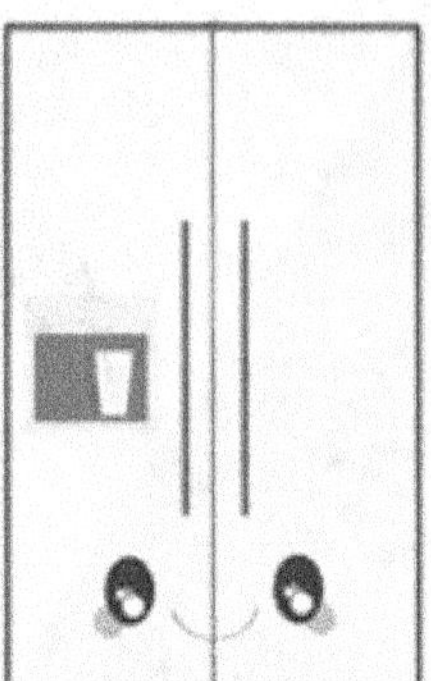

The refrigerator has lots of things inside.

mixeur

mixér

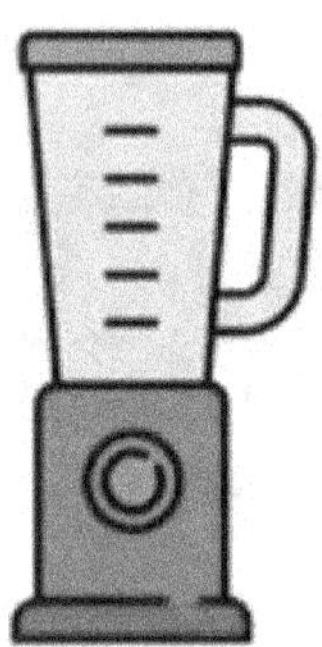

The blender will mix up my fruits.

cabinets

skrine

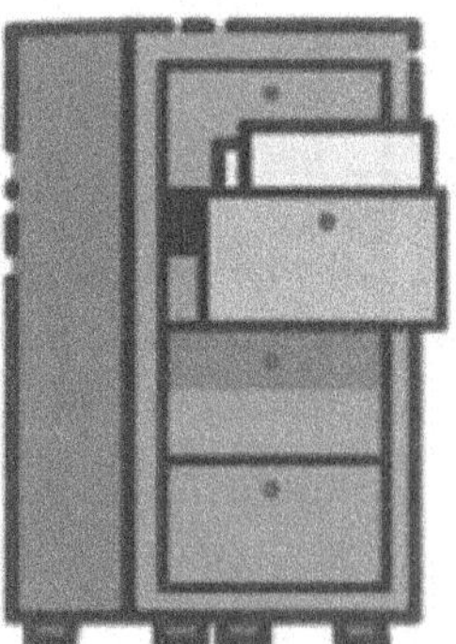

The cabinet has my paper inside.

placard

skriňa

The cupboard has lots of books.

four micro onde

mikrovlnná rúra

The microwave will heat my food.

arrière

spät

She has a slender back.

des joues

tváre

She kisses her mom on the cheek.

poitrine

hruď

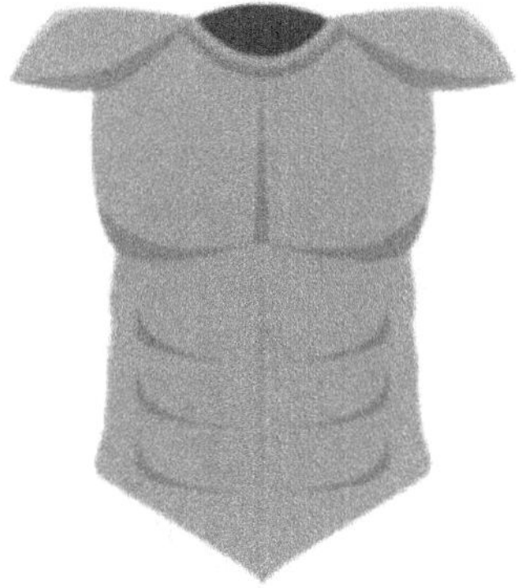

The armor is for your chest.

menton

brada

This is my chin!

oreilles

uši

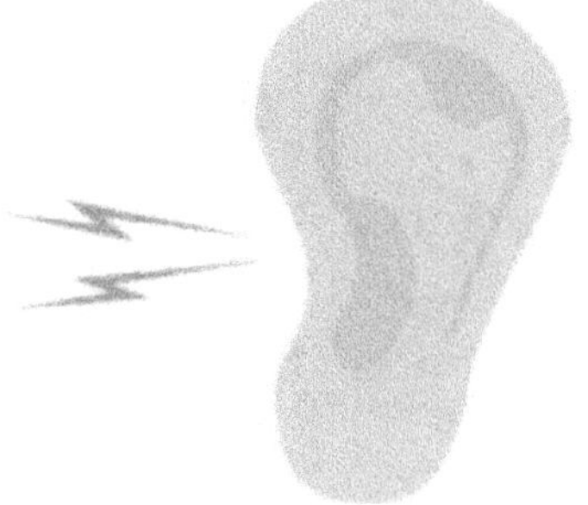

The ear is hearing something.

les sourcils

obočie

The eyebrows are raised.

yeux

oči

The eyes are blue.

pieds

chodidlá

I have one pair of feet.

des doigts

prsty

The fingers are waving at us.

pied

noha

My foot has five fingers.

front

čelo

My brain is behind my forehead.

cheveux

vlasy

My hair is long and black.

mains

ruky

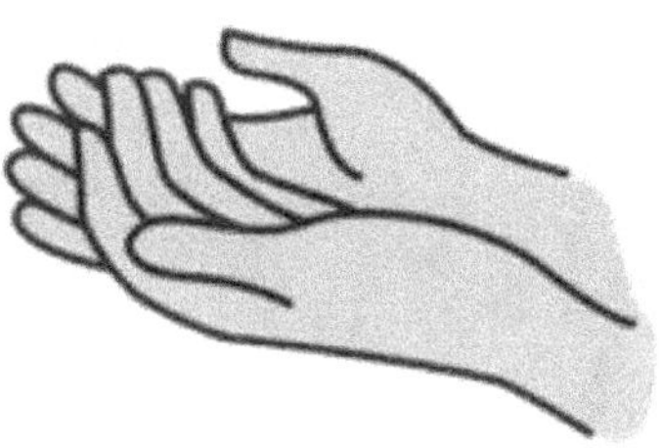

I will wash my hands in the sink.

tête

hlava

She has a big head.

les hanches

boky

The gorilla has his hands on his hips.

les genoux

kolená

She is begging on her knees.

jambes

nohy

The tiger has strong legs.

lèvres

pery

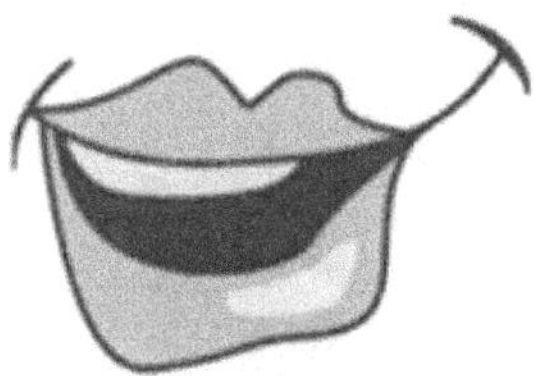

The lips have lipstick on.

bouche

ústa

He is covering his mouth with his hand.

cou

krk

The necklace is very special to me.

nez

nos

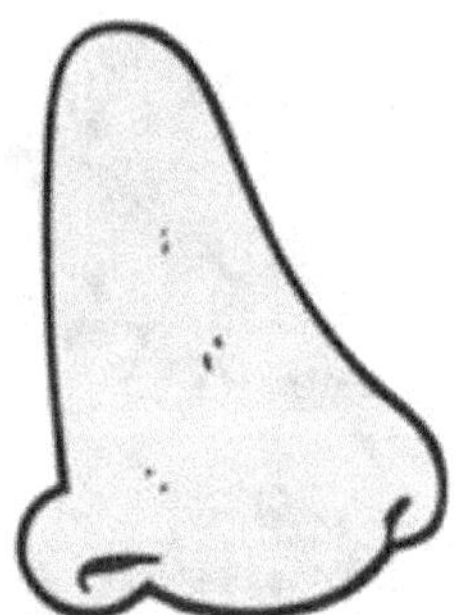

The nose smells something.

épaules

ramená

He puts his hands on his shoulders.

estomac

žalúdok

He has a big stomach.

les dents

zuby

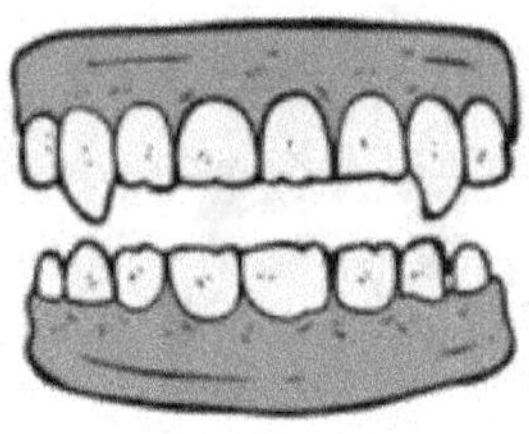

The teeth are clean and white.

gorge

hrdlo

He has a sore throat today.

les orteils

prsty

My toes are small.

langue

jazyk

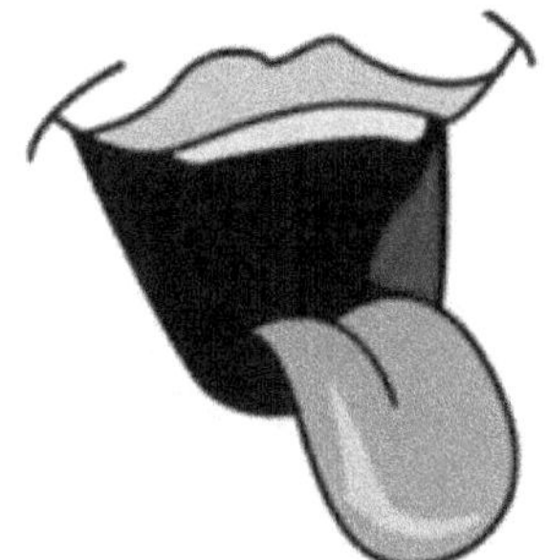

My tongue is licking ice cream.

dent

zub

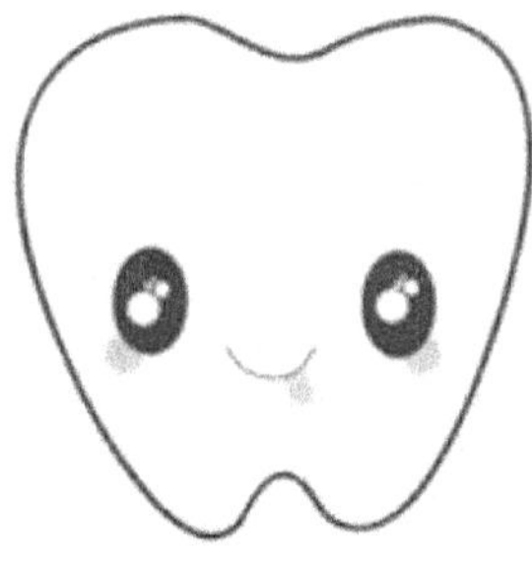

The tooth has big eyes.

taille

pás

He has his hands on his waist.

salopette

kombinéza

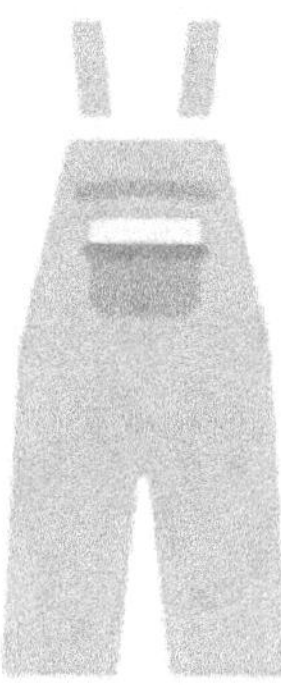

I bought these overalls for you!

mitaines

palčiaky

The mittens are very warm.

bonnet

beanie

The beanie is for winter.

tablier

zástera

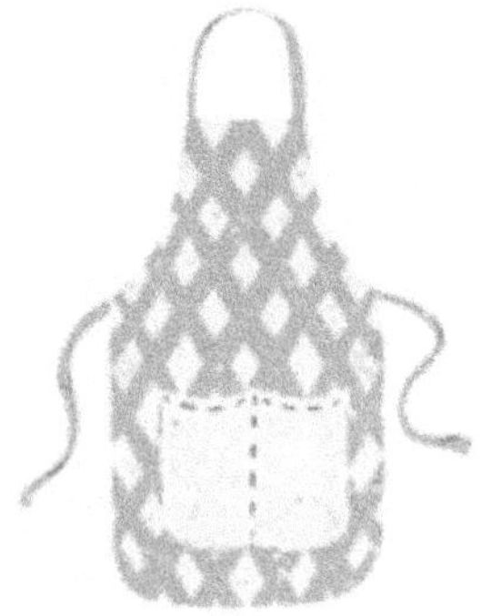

I wear my apron when I bake.

poupée

bábika

The doll is for my baby sister.

hochets

hrkálky

The rattle is for the baby.

jouet

hračka

The toy is very fun.

couche

plienka

The baby has to wear a diaper.

berceau

detský kôš

She is sleeping in her bassinet.

bavoir

podbradník

My baby brother has to wear his
bib when he is eating.

octogone

osemuholník

The octagon is saying okay!

triangle

trojuholník

The triangle has three corners.

carré

námestie

Square

The square has four sides.

cercle

kružnice

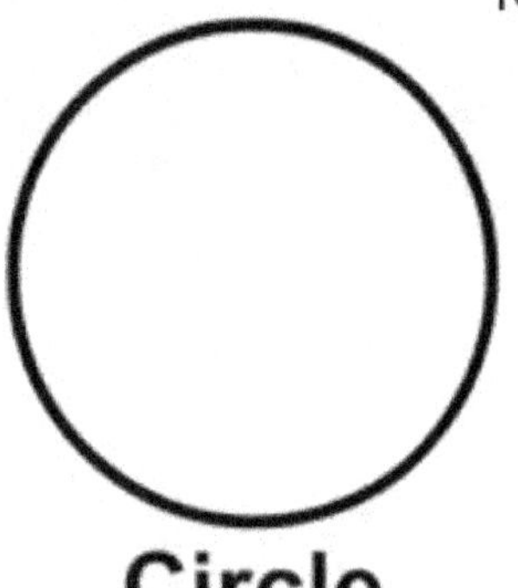

Circle

The circle is round.

ovale

ovál

The oval shape looks like a circle.

cœur

srdce

I drew a heart on my paper.

traverser

kríž

That sign is a cross.

la flèche

arrow

The arrow is pointing this way.

cube

kocky

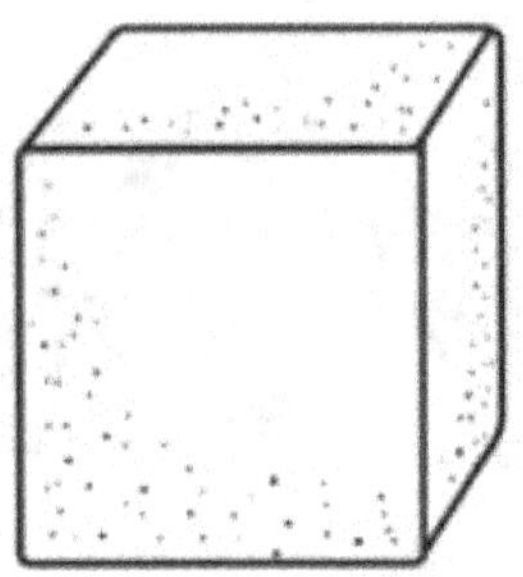

The cube is 3D.

étoile

hviezda

The star is yellow and shiny.

tir à l'arc

lukostreľba

The archery is where you aim.

badminton

badminton

My favorite sport is badminton.

criquet

kriket

I am very good at cricket.

bowling

kolky

I got one pin down at bowling!

boxe

box

The boxing gloves are hot.

tennis

tenis

He can hit the ball in tennis.

faire de la planche a roulettes

skateboarding

He skateboards to school.

planche de surf

surfboarding

The shark loves surfing in the ocean.

le hockey

hokej

I like to play Ice hockey.

yoga

jóga

He is closing his eyes and doing yoga.

épée

šerm

They are fencing and dueling together.

aptitude

vhodnosť

She will do some fitness in the pool.

gymnastique

gymnastika

He can do brilliant gymnastics.

karaté

karate

She is good at kicking in Karate.

volley-ball

volejbal

She is holding a volleyball.

musculation

zdvíhať závažia

The girl with brown hair can do weightlifting.

basketball

basketbal

He can balance the ball with one finger in basketball.

base-ball

baseball

The little chick is in the finales at baseball.

le rugby

ragby

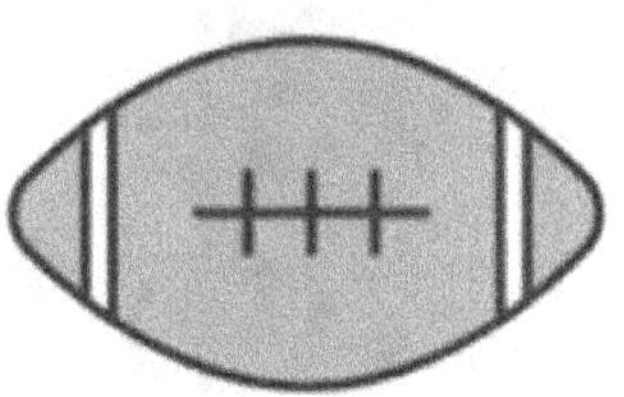

The rugby ball has white stripes.

lutte

zápas

The sumo will compete in wrestling.

course de voitures

automobilové preteky

He is number one for car racing.

cyclisme

jazda na bicykli

He is peacefully cycling on the road.

fonctionnement

beh

He is running while listening to his earphones.

tennis de table

stolný tenis

My brother and dad will play table tennis.

pêche

rybárčenie

He will go to the river to fish.

judo

džudo

She has a red belt in Judo.

escalade

šplhanie

He will climb the ladder.

tournage

streľba

He is shooting the archery board.

le golf

golf

She is going to compete in the golf competition.

balade

jazda

He will ride his scooter.

asseyez-vous

posaď sa

They are sitting down together.

se lever

postaviť sa

She likes to stand up.

bats toi

boj

They are fighting over the book.

rire

smiech

He is laughing so hard!

lis

čítať

She read a picture book.

jouer

hrať

He went to play on the slide.

ecoutez

počúvať

He listened for the ice cream cart.

pleurer

výkrik

He cried because he got a bad grade.

pense

myslieť si

He thought that the test would be hard.

chanter

sing

He sang for the concert.

regarder la télévision

pozerať tv

He watched TV the whole night.

danse

tanec

She was a good dancer.

allumer

zapnúť

The light is turned on.

éteindre

vypnúť

The light is turned off.

gagner

vyhrať

He won the contest.

mouche

fly

The parrot can fly.

couper

rez

He was cutting his nails.

désinvolte

zahodiť

He threw away the garbage.

dormir

spánok

He slept soundly.

fermer

zavrieť

He closed his mouth shut.

ouvert

otvorené

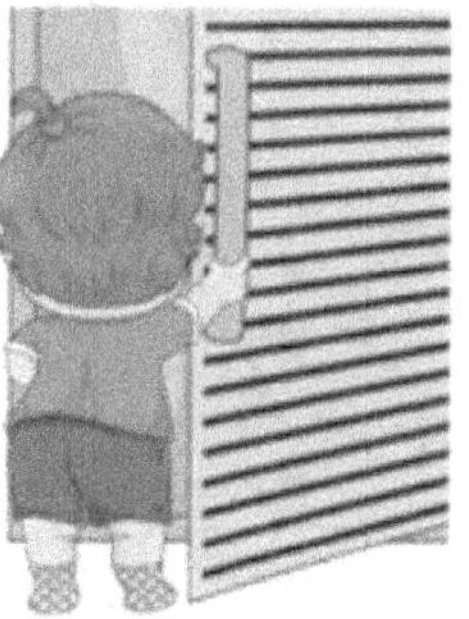

She opened the bathroom door.

écrire

write

She wrote with a pencil.

donner

dať

Santa gave her a present.

sauter

jump

She had fun jumping.

manger

jesť

The shark ate yummy ice cream.

boisson

piť

The old British man drank tea.

cuisinier

kuchár

The microwave cooked his soup.

lavage

umývanie

You need to remember to wash your hands.

attendre

wait

He was waiting for the bus.

montée

šplhať

She climbed a lot of mountains.

parler

rozprávanie

Two best friends were talking together.

crawl

kraul

The baby crawled on the floor.

rêver

snívať

The Sloth dreamed about eating leaves.

creuser

kopať

That strong man dug a swimming pool.

taper

tlieskanie

The baby clapped her hands.

tricoter

pliesť

She knits with the purple string.

coudre

šiť

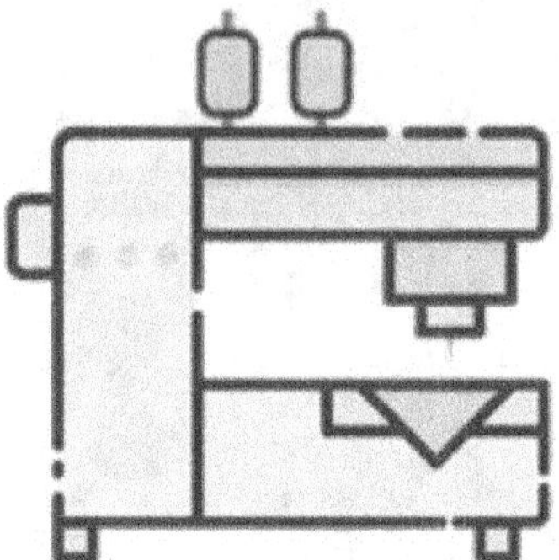

That is a sewing machine.

odeur

vôňa

The perfume smelled great.

baiser

bozk

He kissed his mother.

étreinte

objatie

They hugged each other.

ronfler

chrápanie

The tiger snored.

baigner

kúpať sa

He took a bath.

s'incliner

poklonenie sa

He bowed to the judge.

peindre

maľovať

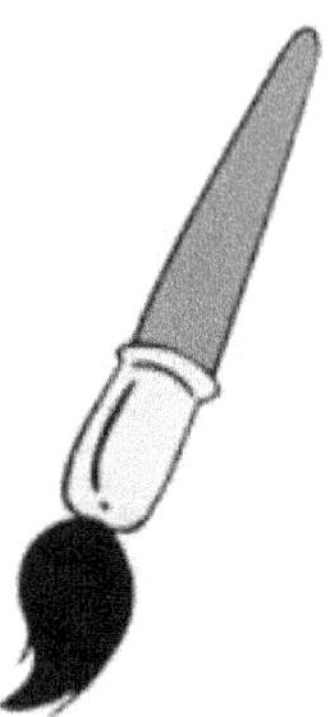

He painted a colorful picture.

se plonger

ponoriť

He dove to the deepest part of the ocean.

ski

lyže

The ski was expensive.

empiler

stoh

The books are stacked high.

acheter

kúpiť

They bought cereal.

secouer

triasť

They shook hands together.

programmeur

programátor

He was a smart computer programmer.

vétérinaire

veterinár

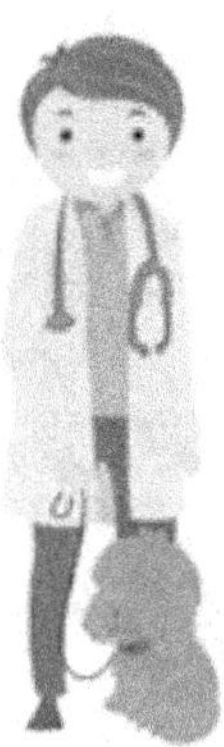

She is a veterinarian.

vendeur de rue

pouličný predavač

That street vendor sells hot dogs.

mineur

baník

That Miner will find gold.

prof

učiteľ

The owl is the teacher.

groom

hotelový poslíček

That Bellboy is fat.

orateur

rečník

The chicken is a great Speaker.

boucher

mäsiar

The Butcher sells fish.

pharmacien

lekárnik

That Pharmacist saved a person's life.

réceptionniste

recepčný

He is a Receptionist.

politicien

politík

He wants to be a Politician.

guide touristique

turistický sprievodca

That Tour guide led us around Japan.

entrepreneur

podnikateľ

He is an Entrepreneur.

danseuse de ballet

baletný tanečník

She is training to be a Ballet dancer.

astronaute

astronaut

He is a great astronaut.

juge

sudca

That Judge is always fair.

avocat

právnik

The lawyer is serious.

la caissière

pokladničné

She is a cashier at the market.

conducteur de taxi

taxikár

He is a fast Taxi driver.

plombier

inštalatér

That Plumber fixes toilets.

musicien

hudobník

She wants to be a Musician like her teacher.

chef

šéfkuchár

The chef makes fast food.

boulanger

pekár

That baker is a bread.

artiste

umelec

That Artist came from Italy.

acteur

herec

That actor is famous.

barman

barman

The Bartender works in a bar.

coiffeur

kaderník

That girl is a Hairdresser.

évêques

biskupi

He is a Bishop.

opticien

optik

She went to an Optician.

fleuriste

kvetinár

She is a great Florist.

écrivain

spisovateľ

He is a famous author.

comptable

účtovný

My accountant is loyal.

du vin

víno

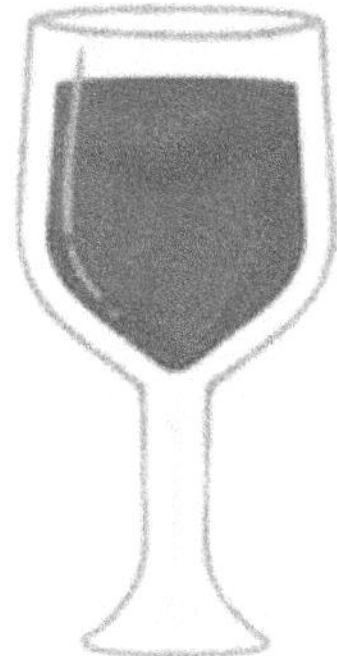

That wine tastes good.

café

káva

That coffee is bitter.

limonade

limonáda

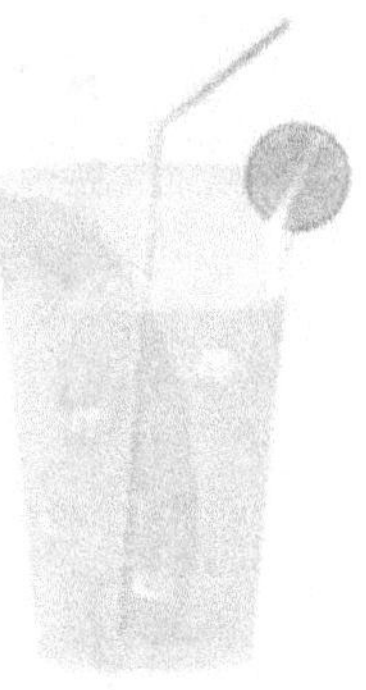

The lemonade is refreshing.

chocolat chaud

horúca čokoláda

I drink hot chocolate every day.

milk-shake

milkshake

The milkshake has whipped cream.

eau

voda

The water is not cold.

thé

čaj

The tea is hot.

lait

mlieko

Milk is white.

bière

pivo

The beer is foamy.

un soda

sóda

The soda is fizzy.

smoothie

smoothie

The smoothie is a watermelon flavor.

milk-shake

milkshake

The milkshake has whipped cream.

lait de coco

kokosové mlieko

The coconut milk is yummy.

du jus d'orange

pomarančový džús

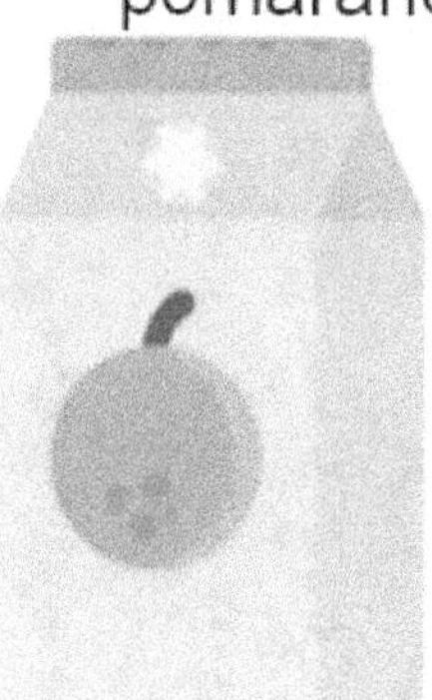

The orange juice is made from oranges.

cacao

kakao

The cocoa is sweet.

fromage

syr

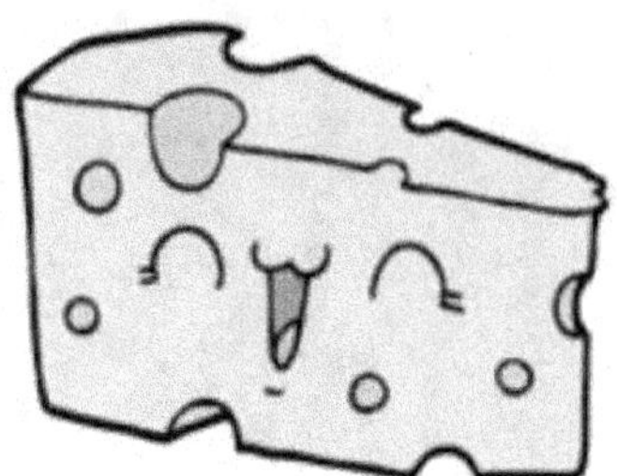

The cheese is creamy.

oeuf

vajíčko

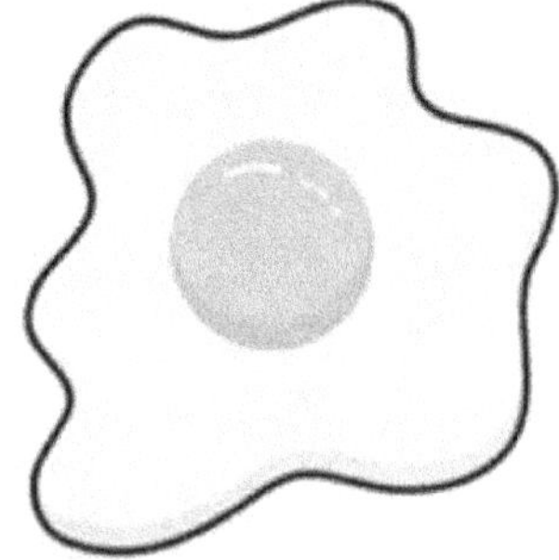

The egg is fried.

beurre

maslo

The butter is put on bread.

margarine

margarín

Margarine looks like butter.

yaourt

jogurt

That yogurt is popular.

cottage cheese

tvaroh

The cottage cheese is put on crackers.

crème glacée

zmrzlina

They have a triple scoop ice cream.

crème

krém

That is a lot of creams.

sandwich

sendvič

That sandwich is healthy.

saucisse

klobása

Americans love sausages.

hamburger

hamburger

That hamburger looks happy.

hot-dog

párok v rožku

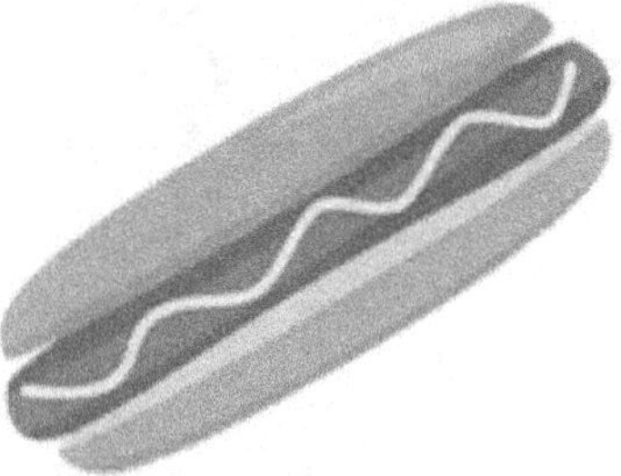

That hot dog has mustard on it.

pain

chlieb

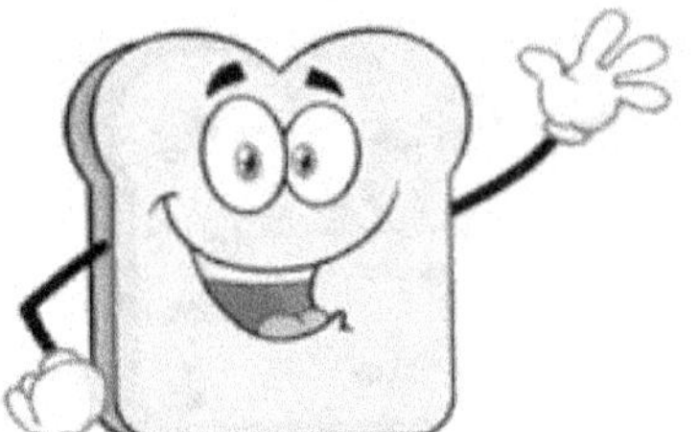

That bread is saying hello.

pizza

pizza

That pizza is cheesy.

steak

steak

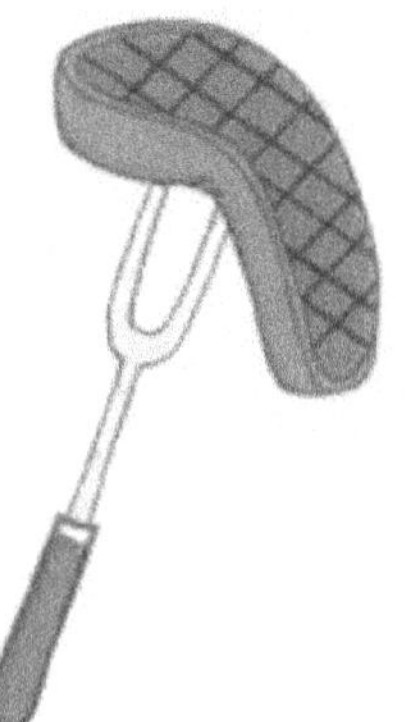

The steak was grilled.

poulet rôti

pečené kura

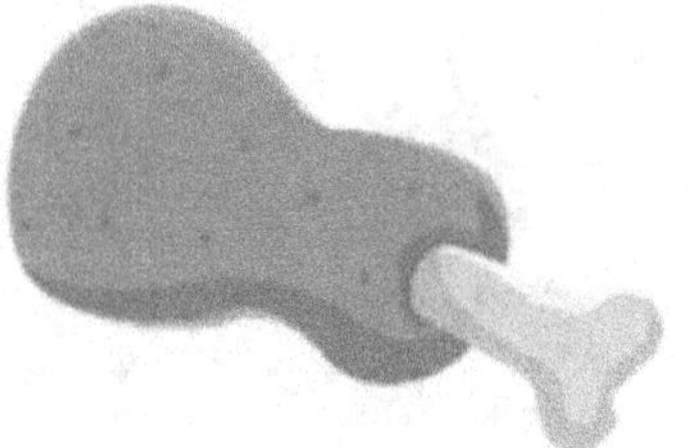

Roast Chicken is delicious.

poisson

ryby

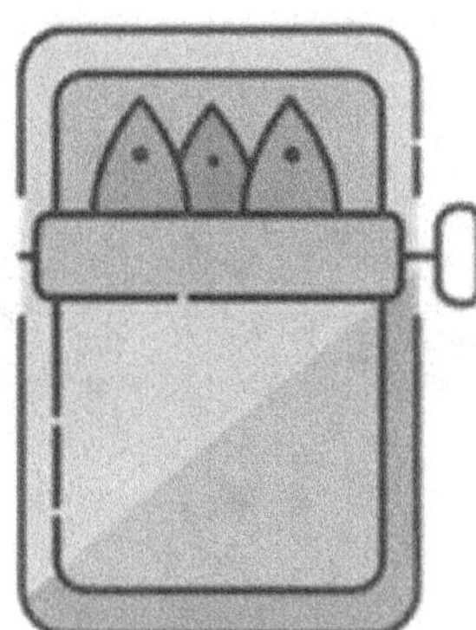

You can buy canned fish in the market.

fruit de mer

morské plody

Lobster is expensive seafood.

jambon

šunka

Ham can be put in sandwiches.

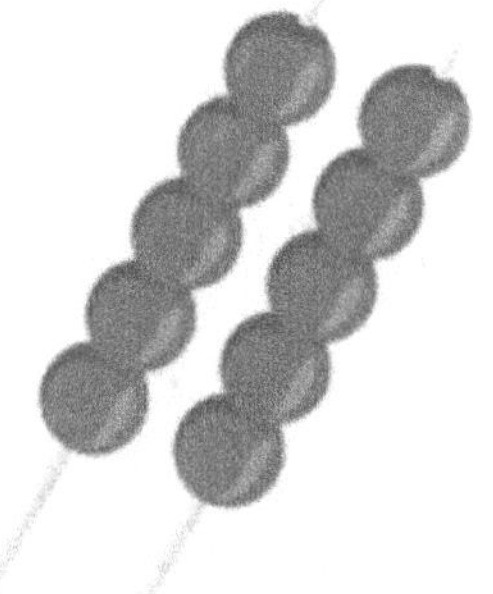

kebab

kebab

Kebab is a delicacy in America.

bacon

slanina

That bacon is smiling.

crème fraîche

kyslá smotana

You can dip your chips in sour cream.

vache

krava

Cows are black and white.

lapin

králik

That rabbit is fun to play with.

canard

kačica

That duck is content.

crevette

garnát

The shrimp has six legs.

porc

prasa

That pig is pink and fat.

abeille

včela

The bee has a stinger.

chèvre

koza

That goat has a white horn.

crabe

krab

The crab has two big pincers.

cerf

jeleň

That deer is sleeping.

dinde

turecko

The turkey has a giant tail.

colombe

holubica

That dove is carrying a plant.

mouton

ovce

That sheep has fluffy wool.

poisson

ryby

That fish has colorful fins.

poulet

kura

That chicken is waking everybody up.

cheval

kôň

The horse has a red mane.

chaise

stoličky

That wing chair is yellow.

meuble tv

televízny stolík

The TV stand can hold books.

canapé

pohovka

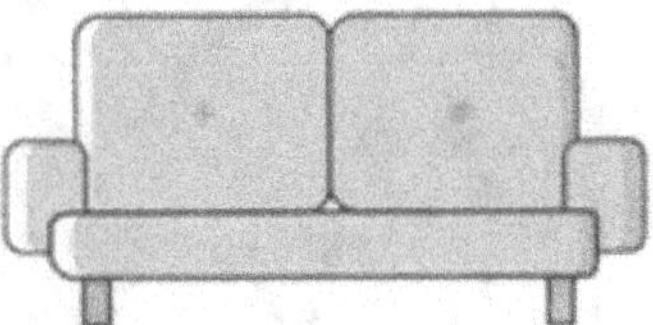

The sofa is comfortable to sit on.

coussins

vankúšiky

The cushion helps soften your seat.

téléphone

telefónne

The telephone is ringing.

télévision

televízia

That television is big.

haut-parleurs

reproduktory

That speaker is used to increase the volume.

table d'appoint

bočný stolík

That end table is sparkling clean.

service à thé

čajová súprava

That tea set is from China.

cheminée

ohnisko

The fireplace makes me warm.

télécommandes

diaľkové ovládače

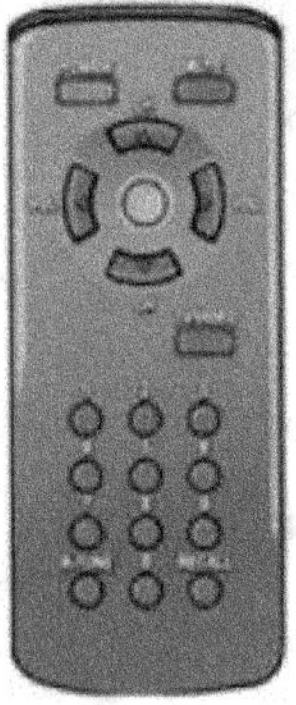

The remote has lots of buttons.

ventilateur électrique

elektrický ventilátor

The fan is blowing wind.

lampadaire

stojaca lampa

The floor lamp is very tall.

tapis

koberec

The carpet is soft and silky.

bureaux

stoly

The table is made of wood.

stores

rolety

I will pull the blinds down.

rideaux

záclony

She opened the curtains.

image

obrázok

The picture is about the mountains and the sky.

vase

váza

The roses are all in a vase.

l'horloge

hodiny

The alarm clock is beeping.

oreiller

vankúš

The pillow is pink and yellow.

cintre

vešiak na klobúky

The hat stand has only one hat on it.

mettre la table

toaletný stolík

I have made up on my dressing table.

lampe de table

stolná lampa

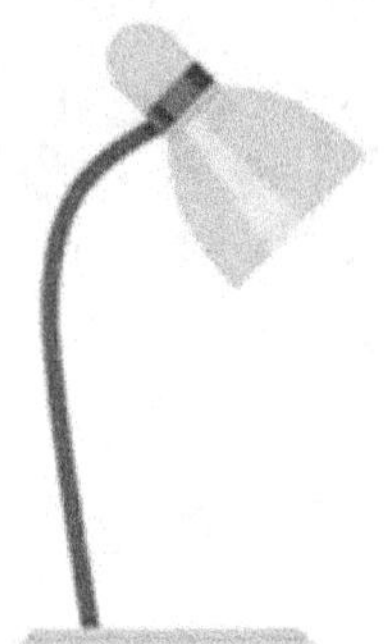

The table lamp will help me see in the dark.

miroir

zrkadlo

The mirror is very tall.

planche a repasser

žehliaca doska

Don't touch the ironing board, it's hot!

boîte avec tiroir

škatuľka so zásuvkou

You can keep your clothes in the hope chest.

table de chevet

nočný stolík

The nightstand has my lamp on it.

lit

posteľ

The bed is charming.

climatisation

klimatizácia

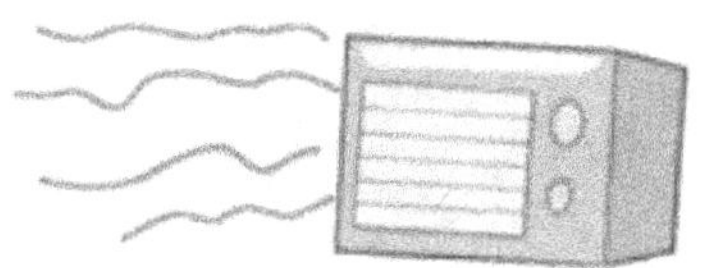

The air conditioner is cold.

cruche

džbán

The measuring jug has nothing inside.

dentifrice

zubná pasta

The toothpaste is mint flavored.

brosse à dents

zubná kefka

The toothbrush has toothpaste on it.

savon

mydlo

The soap is very bubbly.

pince à linge

kolíček

The clothespin will clip my clothes.

cintre

ramienko

The hanger is hanging my boots.

sèche-cheveux

fén

The hairdryer will blow my hair.

shampooing

šampón

The shampoo is used to clean your hair.

bulle

bublina

The bubbles are very fun to play in.

brosse

kefa

She is brushing her hair with the brush.

papier toilette

toaletný papier

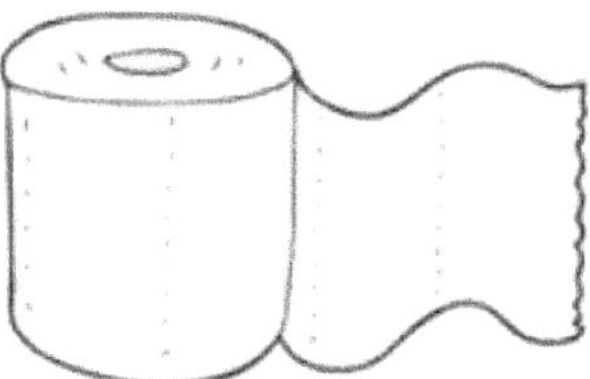

The toilet paper is used to dry your hands.

serviette

uterák

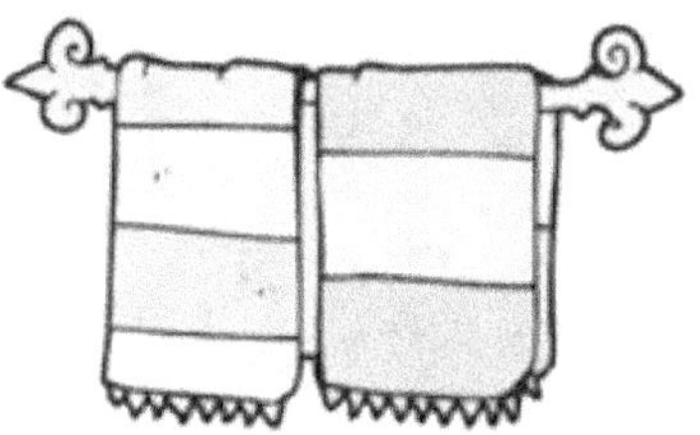

We have two towels on the rack.

corde à linge

bielizeň

My shirt is hanging on the clothesline.

douche

sprcha

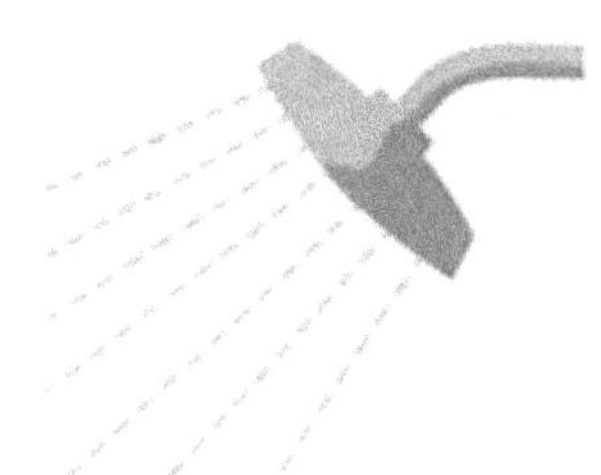

The shower is spraying water.

baignoire

vaňa

The bathtub is comfortable.

lessive

pracích práškov

The laundry detergent is used with the washing machine.

seau

vedro

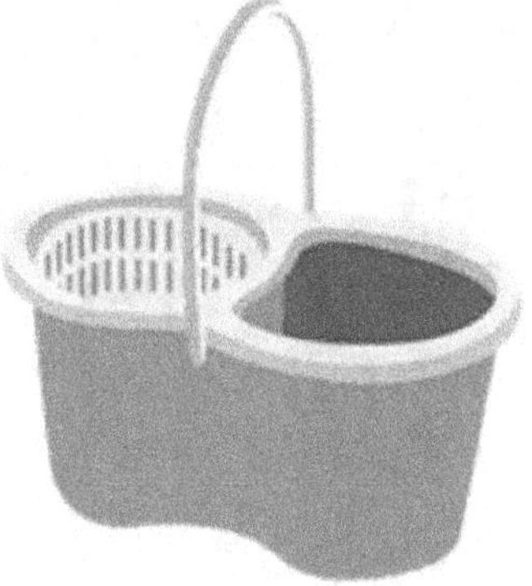

Can you help me fill up the bucket?

vadrouilles

mopy

The mop is used for mopping the floor.

savon liquide

tekuté mydlo

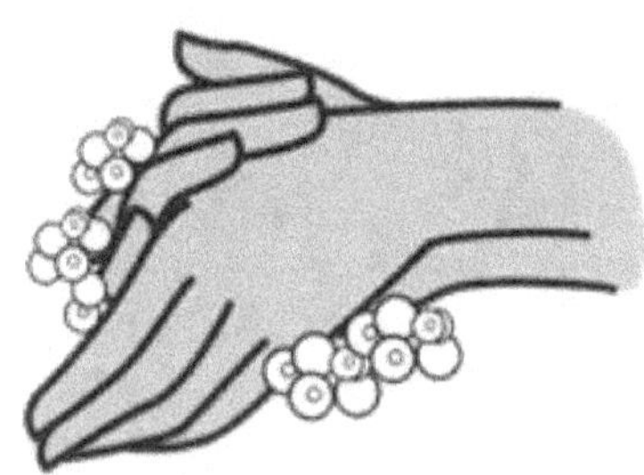

I use soapy water to wash my hands.

lessive en poudre

prací prášok

I will scoop up the washing powder.

sac poubelle

vrece na odpadky

The trash bag is full of trash.

poubelle

odpadkový kôš

You have only to put recylcle trash in the trash can.

les puits

drezy

You should wash your hands in the sink.

cuvette des toilettes

záchodová misa

She let her bunny use the toilet.

machine à laver

práčka

The washing machine wash your clothes.

panier à linge

kôš na bielizeň

She is putting all the clothes into the laundry basket.

le rasoir

britva

He uses the razor to shave his beard.

rasoir électrique

elektrický holiaci strojček

The electric razor works faster than the normal one.

crème à raser

krém na holenie

The shaving cream is fluffy.

bain de bouche

ústna voda

The mouthwash smells very lovely.

coton-tige

vatová tyčinka

Q-tip can be used for many things.

brosse à cheveux

kefa na vlasy

She brushes her hair with her hairbrush.

peigne

hrebeň

Her dad will comb her hair for her.

nettoyant

čističi

Put the cap back on the cleanser bottle.

échelle

mierka

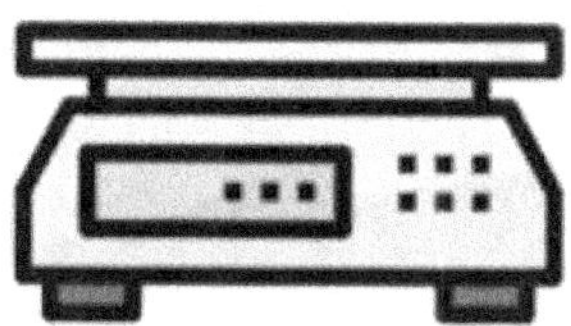

You can measure things on the scale.

papier de soie

vreckovka

The tissue is on the counter.

jouets de bain

hračky do kúpeľa

The little duck is a bath toy.

robinet

kohútik

The faucet is broken.

miroir

zrkadlo

He is looking in the mirror.

tapis de bain

kúpeľňa koberec

The bath mat is purple and yellow.